The Pets Are Wonderful Family Album

The Pets Are Wonderful Family Album

THE PETS ARE
WONDERFUL COUNCIL

PREFACE BY
Betty White

G. P. PUTNAM'S SONS
New York

Line from "The Pangolin" is reprinted with permission of
Macmillan Publishing Company from *The Collected Poems of
Marianne Moore*. Copyright 1941, and renewed 1969, by
Marianne Moore.

Book design by Dorothy Wachtenheim

Library of Congress Cataloging in Publication Data

Main entry under title:

The Pets Are Wonderful family album.

1. Pets—Pictorial works. I. Pets Are Wonderful Council.
SF416.5.P48   1984   779'.32   84-9831
ISBN 0-399-12980-4

Printed in the United States of America

PREFACE
by
Betty White

Is it just me, or do you sometimes get the feeling we are living under a perpetual barrage of rule changes?

What was yesterday's health diet becomes today's poison. What was supposed to be a great exercise program is suddenly fraught with hidden perils. And as far as advice on bringing up children is concerned, the pendulum no longer just swings back and forth, but seems to go in full circles.

No doubt it has always been this way, and only the tempo has accelerated, but it leaves us with a tremendous longing for something with a degree of constancy . . . something that can be depended upon *not* to change.

Take heart. The following pages contain comforting examples of just that constancy. The pictures included here could have been taken any time, any place throughout history, and the essence would be exactly the same—the remarkable invisible bond between pets and people.

Everyone who views these photographs will enjoy them, but all see them differently, on our own personal level. And this I guarantee: for each of us there will be that very special one that strikes home so intensely it's as if we were part of the picture.

Sit back, relax, and enjoy the feeling. Which is *your* picture? I know mine.

INTRODUCTION

The Pets Are Wonderful (PAW) Council is a national, not-for-profit, public service organization dedicated to promoting one message: having a pet is a joyful and rewarding experience. We serve as a source of pet news and information, and we sponsor special education and community relations programs to demonstrate the many ways that dogs and cats contribute to our well-being and happiness.

One of our most successful efforts was a national photography contest sponsored in cooperation with *Family Circle* Magazine. In an overwhelming response, more than 25,000 Americans from coast to coast flooded the Pets are Wonderful Council with an astonishing variety of photographs. Some are beautiful and touching, others are humorous and heartwarming, all of them picture the friendship and love that exists between families and their dogs and cats. Entrants in the "Pets Are Part of Your Family Circle" photo contest were asked to capture this special relationship on film. And they did just that. We received photos that eloquently expressed that unique bond and now, with *The Pets Are Wonderful Family Album*, we have a rare opportunity to share them with you. Along with the 53 prize-winning photographs from the contest, we have included many of the runners-up—a loving display that demonstrates just how important and strong these bonds of friendship are.

Here are photographs that make it dramatically clear that dogs and cats provide affection, security and an overall sense of well-being to every member of the family. In picture after picture we see love mutually given, and there can be no doubt that pets really are best friends and close members of the family.

That dogs and cats make many significant contributions to our lives is something that has been known to pet owners for years. Pets provide us with physical and psychological benefits that enrich the quality of our lives from infancy to old age. In addition to the years of loyal companionship and uncritical love and acceptance that people receive from their pets, studies have shown that stroking a cat or a dog can lower blood pressure and reduce heart rate, helping to relieve the stresses of busy adults and growing children. You will see many photos in which a sleeping dog or dozing cat provides a "snuggling" moment after work or school that eases away the day's tensions.

Again, research has shown that the warm, soft presence of a dog or cat is good for families because it promotes greater interaction, strengthens relationships and increases and improves communication between family members. We received photos showing pets involved in just about every activity imaginable: from the morning shave to the plowing of a field to watching a favorite after-dinner TV program.

Children also benefit from the love and companionship a pet offers. A pet helps the young learn empathy and respect for other living creatures—the child becomes a part of another life's pain and joy. Children can gain greater self-esteem and self-confidence through the care and love of a family pet, and many smart parents know that owning a pet is a wonderful way for them to teach a child responsibility. A pet is also a real, comforting presence to children who come home to an empty house after school because both parents work. Pets help children feel more secure, and in the following pages you will see how truly important a dog or cat is to a child of any age.

But children aren't the only ones who benefit from owning a pet. Having a dog or a cat is a simple way for a young couple to experience the joys of interacting with a creature dependent on their love who can respond with love in turn. Pets also provide companionship for the elderly at a time in their lives when they might otherwise be alone and lonely.

As the camera shows, cats and dogs are a part of the workplace as well. People across the country make their pets a part of their workday. Hairdressers, farmers, auto mechanics, seamstresses and accountants were just a few of the many folks who sent us photos of their dogs and cats on the job.

Of course pets are also involved when people are having a good time. We've featured action-filled shots of people and their pets at play: at the beach, in the mountains, at home, even at the club—on the tennis court naturally! Another benefit of owning pets, especially dogs, is that they encourage their owners to exercise and pursue a more active and healthful life. If the photos are any indication, Americans from San Francisco Bay to Boston Harbor are walking, running, swimming, rafting, fishing, hiking, motor-cycling, roller skating and even skiing with their dogs and cats.

While people are out with their pets, they're also meeting others and making new friends. It's a fact that people are more inclined to approach a stranger with a dog than someone alone—pets are great conversation starters! Almost every pet owner has had the experience of having someone stop to pet his dog or stroke his cat, prompting compliments and an exchange of stories—instant friendships that bring people together for a moment or a lifetime.

More and more people see their pets as friends and members of the family—unfailing companions that are a comfort and joy to children and adults alike and who help us live happier, healthier, even longer lives. In a world filled with change and uncertainty, our relationship with our pets remains a constant comfort, for they are our friends who give and receive love without question or complaint. The heartwarming photographs on the following pages are dramatic proof of these sentiments—pets are wonderful!

The
Pets Are
Wonderful
Family
Album

"A dog is the only thing on this earth that loves you more than he loves himself."

Josh Billings

"Sometimes children feel themselves more akin to animals than to their elders."

Sigmund Freud

"Pets always seem to know what a person is feeling."
Betty White

"... in life
the firmest
friend,
the first
to welcome,
foremost to
defend."

Lord Byron

"A dog is like a liberal. He wants to please everybody."

William Kunstler

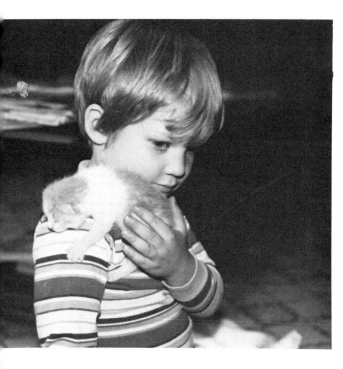

"Nay, brother of the sod,
What part hast thou in God?
What spirit art thou of?
It answers, Love."

Katharine Lee Bates

"A faithful friend is a strong defense: and he who hath found such a one hath found a treasure."

from the Apocrypha

"Thou unassuming commonplace of Nature . . ."
William Wordsworth

"Every dog (and cat)
has his day . . ."
George Borrow

"Not what we give, but what we share . . ."

James Russell Lowell

"Ye are better than all the ballads that ever were sung or said . . ."
Henry Wadsworth Longfellow

"One word frees us of all the weight and pain of life:
That word is love."

Sophocles

"Histories are more full of examples of the fidelity of dogs than of friends."

Alexander Pope

"To him who in the love of Nature holds communion with her visible forms, she speaks a various language."

William Cullen Bryant

"When you're special to a cat, you're special indeed . . . she brings to you the gift of her preference of you, the sight of you, the sound of your voice, the touch of your hand."

Leonore Fleischer

"When I play with my cat,
who knows whether I do not
amuse her more than
she amuses me."

Montaigne

"I have never found in a human being loyalty that compared to that of any pet."

Doris Day

"A little work, a little play, to keep us going, and so good day!"

George du Maurier

"The one absolutely unselfish friend that man can have in this selfish world, the one that never deserts him, the one that never proves ungrateful or treacherous, is his dog."

George Graham Vest

"I think I could turn and live with animals, they are so placid and self-contained . . ."

Walt Whitman

"Let sleeping dogs lie . . ."
Charles Dickens

"One might think Nature had given animals to us as a lesson in good living."

Plutarch

"The heart of animals is the foundation of their life . . ."
William Harvey

"I had rather see the portrait of a dog I know than all the allegorical paintings they can show me in the world."

Samuel Johnson

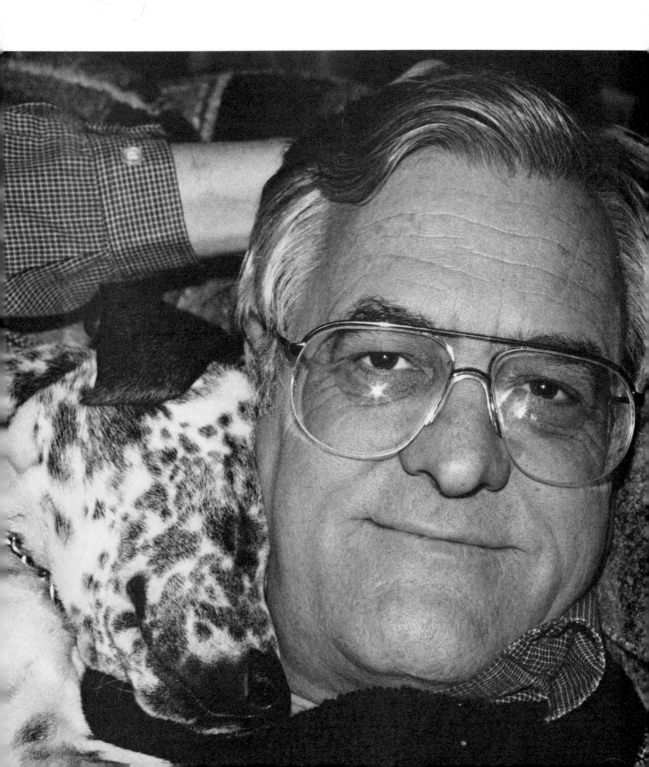

"A faithful
friend is
the medicine
of life."

Anonymous

"The bond between people and pets supplements what is available in human relationships. It satisfies our need to nurture."

Bruce Fogle

"A very gentle beast and of good conscience."
William Shakespeare

"In all things of nature there is something of the marvelous."
Aristotle

"Perhaps there is no
happiness in life
so perfect . . ."

O. Henry

"A dog teaches a boy fidelity, perseverance, and to turn around three times before lying down."

Robert Benchley

"Pets are as much a part of most people's lives as their own human kin."   Michael Fox, D.V.M.

"Take a good look into the eyes of your dog. If you don't see what I see, then spell dog backwards."

Dr. Frank Vigue

"Among animals one has a sense of humor."
Marianne Moore

"Friends share all things."
Pythagoras

"Little friend of all the world."
Rudyard Kipling

"Animals are such agreeable friends—they ask no questions, they pass no criticisms."

George Eliot

"A good dog–person match is a gift of the heavens."
Roger Caras

"They that ever mind the world
to win/must have a black cat, a
howling dog, and a crowing hen."

Proverb

"The health of people and their animals is really the foundation upon which their happiness and their powers as a State depend."

Benjamin Disraeli

"He's gentle, he is kind; I'll never, never find a better friend than old dog Tray."

Stephen Collins Foster

"The best mirror is an old friend."
George Herbert

"A little season of love and laughter . . ."
Adam Lindsay Gordon

"Grow old along with me! The best is yet to be . . ."
Robert Browning

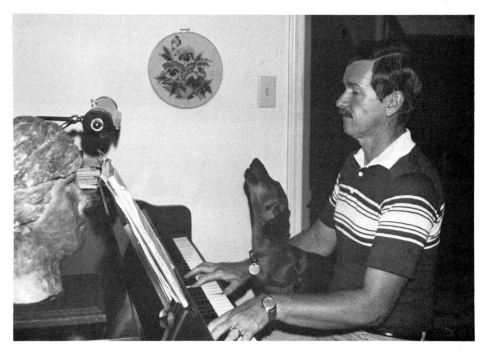

"He loves to sit and hear me sing then laughing, sports and plays with me . . ."

William Blake

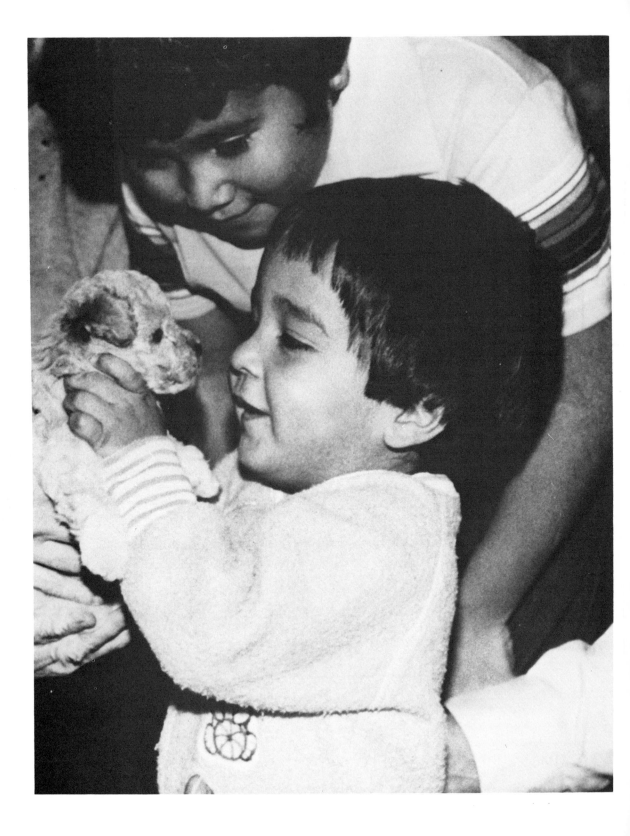

"You can tell by the kindness of a dog how the human should be."

Captain Beefheart

"Two dogs of black, St. Hubert's breed,
unmatched for courage, breadth and speed."
Sir Walter Scott

"What is man without the beasts? If all the beasts were gone man would die from great loneliness of the spirit, for whatever happens to the beasts also happens to the man."

Seattle of the Duwanish Tribe

"Beauty unadorned."

Aphta Behn

"All are but parts of one stupendous whole,
Whose body Nature is, and God the soul."

Alexander Pope

"Nature teaches beasts to know his friends."
William Shakespeare

"My little old dog: A heart-beat at my feet."
Edith Wharton

"The great pleasure of a dog is that you may make a fool of yourself
with him and not only will he not scold you, but he will make
a fool of himself too."

Samuel Butler

"A cat is restfulness; it's impossible not to relax in the presence of a dozing cat."

Leonore Fleischer